"Through the whole spectrum of human development, its puzzles, pain, and poetry, Jan Elpel nods to mystery. Singular in its story and reflections, we see the emergence of a Self, multifaceted, mercurial, wild, and free."
       Linda Welsh, author *of Facing the Mountain*

"Jan Elpel's extensive knowledge of the psyche, her spiritual depth, and creative genius shine brightly in these soulful journal entries and poems. Beautifully rendered and thought provoking."
    Connie Myslik-McFadden, Jungian-oriented psychotherapist
      and author of *The Second Bucket List* and *Willow's Gift*

"*Journals of the Psyche* by Dr. Jan Elpel offers her exploration of ever-deepening self-awareness through her gifts of creative expression. Using poetry and art—not linear memories or personal narrative—she has plumbed the depths through both Word and Image. The artistic images express a range of these aspects of the Self (versus ego): use of bold contrasting colors suggest a growing "core" of internal awareness; a mandala made of rocks create a "spiral jetty" (reminiscent of nature artist Goldsworthy): a classic more Jungian mandala of a beautiful 4-quadrant circle—the common symbol of Wholeness; and an image of a lone tree devoid of leaves but strong in gnarled trunk and roots, a powerful metaphor for a full life lived through seasons of both growth and decay. Elpel seeks new possibilities and an ongoing "recreation" of Self through Words and the Images they evoke."
       Eugenia Funk, Ph.D., Clinical Psychologist

Publisher HOPS PRESS, LLC, 2024
Graphic Design and Layout by GRIFFIN
Art and Illustrations by Jan Elpel
Stone Spirals by Cherie Elpel
Lone Tree & Steel Spiral by Dixie Jewett
                       All Rights Reserved, Copyright 2024

ISBN: 978-1-892784-54-4
Author Jan Elpel, PSY.D.
Poetry, Mystical, Mythological, Spiritual
Psychological, Psychoanalytical

                    Silver Sage Studio & Press
                    Bozeman, Montana 59718

To Ingeborg and Susan

in Gratitude for Journeying with Me

Illustrated
JOURNALS OF THE PSYCHE
&
Collected Poems

JAN ELPEL

The human psyche is always full of new possibilities.
It is constantly re-creating itself, and
is perpetually being re-created.

Power in the Helping Professions
A. G-Craig, 1971

JOURNALS OF THE PSYCHE
The Thrust for Individuation

    Psyche and Self

    Psyche and Love

    Psyche and Creativity

    Psyche and Shadow

    Psyche and Soul

    Psyche and Healing

    Psyche and Suffering

    Psyche and the Unconscious

    Psyche and Muse

    Psyche and Poetry

    Psyche and Destiny

    Psyche and Death

JOURNALS CONTENTS

I.	Stirrings		XVI.	Reflections
II.	Discovering		XVII.	Bravo
II.	Psyche		XVIII.	Puzzling
IV.	Shadow		XIX.	Pain
V.	Universal		XX.	Destiny
VI.	Heros		XXI.	Poetry
VII.	Dreams		XXII.	Soul
VIII.	Cosmic		XXIII.	Authenticity
IX.	Godhead		XXIV.	Psyche-Sexual
X.	Creativity		XXV.	Dance
XI.	Beyond		XXVI.	Aloneness
XII.	World		XXVII.	Song
XIII.	Psychosis		XXVIII.	Defenses
XIV.	Existential		XXIX.	Death
XV.	Sovereignty		XXX.	Arriving

HAIKUS FOREVER

&

COLLECTED POEMS

Legacy

Chippings

Did I Dream Sophia?

All the Queen's Horses

The Hijab

I Am Woman

Pilgrimage to Odessa

I Don't Remember

I Don't Remember 2

Musings 1

Musings 2

Musings 3

A Mother Out There

JOURNALS OF THE PSYCHE

.....the psyche writes me

I

STIRRINGS underground, migratory fowl
overhead, seasons' ritual awakenings
dawnings, birth of the world anew
fresh scents scatter on tender breezes.
Spring bulbs awaken, thrust upwards
from deep often unyielding soils
reptiles, foxes, marmots emerge from holes.
Yearnings to be oneself rustle in each of us
a caress at first, a phantom realizing itself
a tulip bulb's bold exertion to be a tulip
not a bougainvillea, a willow sprout a
willow, not a manzanita or wild rose thicket.
Yearnings, quintessential unseen desires
seduce, inveigle and nudge, a veritable
pigsty of shape-shifting Rubic Cubes
confuse, disorient, yet fascinate me.
Uninvited, yet inimitable, they lodge
permanently in the psyche.

II

DISCOVERING the world, initiating

the senses of the newborn, unfocused vision

moving shadows, an aimless reach.

Seven years later my awakening

a stunt pilot crashes on a runway near us

a nose dive, an explosion, a burst of

flames, a column of black oily smoke,

In horror, I whisper, 'A man's in there!

'Don't look,' Daddy cautions from

our perch on the rodeo fence

"Cover your eyes.' He means to

spare us from imprints, psychic terrors,

nightmares, fears and trauma

I peeked through spread fingers

the Self discovering Itself.

III

PSYCHE, mythical, an invisible mystery
science mapped every iota of the mind
literature celebrated the Muse of old
still the greatest frontier lies deeper.
Named in mythology, defined by Freud
applied as user-friendly by Jung
a constant in cave dweller drawings,
in artifacts of faith, rituals, and beliefs.
Yet the concept of Psyche shifted
over time from deity and guide to internal
highjacker, better to know than fail
to acknowledge its shadowy presence
Grand Inquisitor of one's drives, intent,
one's every selfless and self-serving ways
labeling blame on Thee not Me.
Today my creator, my critic, my Muse.

IV

SHADOW, the itinerant instigator
*"I do not understand it, but what I want not
to do I do.'* St. Paul, confounded,
ad libs moral taskmaster consciousness
articulates the psyche, how clever!
Who then is driving the bus?
Moral dilemmas, less for the dogmatic
yet a constancy of an inconstant course
achieves a descent into individual chaos
social breakdown, fascism.gov.
Loop-de-loops, a lop-sided ferris wheel
we counter with games, doomsday videos,
myopic self-analysis, street corner druggies.
Who else but the psyche embraces
this innate corrupting interloper?

V

UNIVERSAL psyche, a life-long wonderment

creativity, a free floating Spirit

I ask, 'Where did that come from?'

enfolding a concept of Creator

the sly and sometimes malevolent Muse.

Psyche, the healer, the spoiler

often appears as the art of self-indulgence

of simmering regret and revenge,

of terminal angst, blind lack of probity

tempered, on the other hand, with

wholesome wisdom of the ancients,

ancestors, indigenous, Asian contemplation

Thich Nhat Hanh for the masses

a consciousness of community, restraint, humility

a quietude, acceptance of yin-yang.

VI

HEROES, each of us prompted by psyche
questing the outer limits of human
imagination, yearnings, again that urge
that makes us willing recruits on the way
to finding Oneself, to grow up and
play Dungeons and Dragons for real.
Yet half a century ago science scorned the
mystical, the inner knowing, the medieval
soothsayers, shamans, clairvoyants,
grandmothers and innocents.
Enlightened these days, psyche sensed as Soul
possessed by all sentient beings, humans,
dogs, cats, and horses, maybe toads and
springboks and June bugs sharing unique caches
of magical whims and urges, mythologies,
playfulness and delight, a mirror reflection.

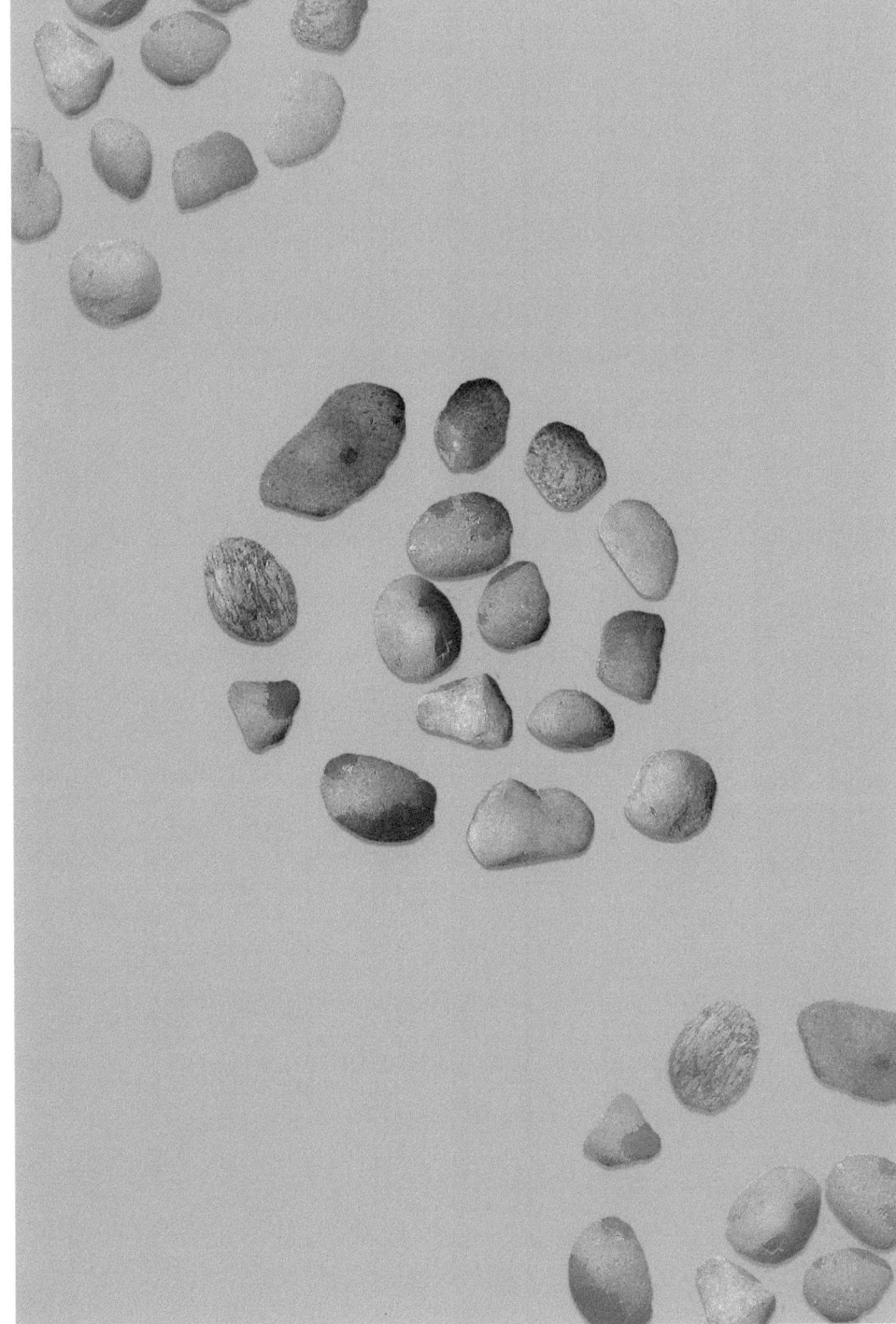

VII

DREAMS, playground of the psyche

retrieval mines its archeology,

psychiatry plunders its dephs, psychology

takes us back to times of Origin

when dreams were sacrosanct, when

Joseph in the desert dreamed his people

home to his father, to forgive his

brothers, a leap of faith in the Holy

Writ of dreams, divinations and visions,

innate to psyches of shamans and witches

and healers, blank slates of projections

of all manner of art and images

revelations and mischief. Day dreams and

night dreams wield the child's paintbrush

and conductor's wand and ballerina leaps

and sculptor's tool. No escapades of the ego

or depths of Spirit escape grist for

dream images and metaphorical dramas.

VIII

COSMIC, the universal consciousness,

the psyche we know, weighed, weighted,

are we better for theories about it?

Times seem unfettered from moral

underpinnings, unruly, resentful, lost dreams,

cities of unsheltered, death by drones, arbitrary

razor wire against the starving, displaced.

How to elevate our higher selves to prize

the home and hearth and till,

enjoy the capacity to mature, safe, secure,

nurture our wisdom nature

mindful the evolving Self defies

genomes and personality quizzes

abides its time on a cosmic journey

of all its people.

IX

GODHEAD, the psyche in every mortal

meet your human ego counterpart,

ego, meet your Sisyphus' Stone

a laughing nymph somewhere

takes note of human drama

evolving, reenacting, reinventing

as if we were the first peoples

yet employing defenses, denials, deadly

confrontations with the ill-defined

creature of the night, the Shadow,

psyche harboring the Divine

the Muse, to Pushkin's delight

in his brightest days writing poetry,

'till a twisted possessiveness

gallantly forced a duel that took the life

of Russia's beloved poet

X

CREATIVITY, first thoughts

untarnished, undeliberate, unspoiled

that inner impulse to scratch marks

on the walls of Kyivan caves

ancient Varangian hieroglyphs

of twelfth century Rus

as in Navaho Monument Valley

finely traced petroglyph stories

etched on high red clay buttes,

grandmothers' wrinkled brown hands

weave ancestral designs into rugs, blankets,

baskets, intuitive, knowing the old ways,

jewelry fashioned from living stone and minerals,

the turquoise and silver bracelets

story telling with each creation.

XI

BEYOND individual unconscious

beyond the gift of awareness,

of instincts and ego and libido

beyond the sheet held up

to play a game of peek-a-boo

lies the deep psychology of society.

Imperceptible on our good days

but given passing time outlines

of a societal psyche emerge in stark relief.

Unfounded fears of intuition, foresight,

inner knowing cast as magical powers,

the Salem witch hunts, banned books and

righteous rules, fears of shamans, midwives,

seeking someone to blame,

to defeat voices of wisdom

behind the ubiquitous sheet.

XII

WORLD'S PSYCHE, reflected in loss

of species, bird and wildlife, overall

a commiserate loss of human psyche's

conscious and unconscious knowing

loss of deep wells of sentience

of integrity of moral beings.

Retrievable with insight, awareness,

changing humankind to be accountable,

to lift up placeholders of wisdom

dance for forgotten rituals

resurrect deep knowing of salmon runs

and lunar seasons of seeding and harvest,

of folklore and visions and dreams.

XIII

PSYCHOSIS, the psyche reclaiming itself
the mind of youth on a heroes journey
a providential mandate for self-preservation,
for rescue from the Big Gulp of identity loss,
a double-edged sword slashes
one's sense of being and knowing
undercuts one's thrust to becoming
invalidates one's feelings, sense of self
on one's journey for confirmation,
let ME be ME!
Heroes psychotic in self-defense
coping with grief and loss, trauma, addictions,
abandonment, somatic imbalance.
Seen as honorable, as adaptive, an inner knowing
guards the gateway to integrity of the psyche.
Rebellion, the peculiarity of going off the rails,
heroes, re-owning one's Self.

XIV

EXISTENTIAL threat, psychic pain
an individual mortal stabbing pain
a bloodless mortal stabbing pain
of loss, lost love, lost self-regard
lost dreams, lost reason to be.
Yearnings, drives, life's energy for being
absconded by a greater desire for non-being
Hemingway's hell personified
let the pain cease, fly me away
a psychic mantra too long denied
ambivalence too long endured
a latent inner impulse of self destruction
underlies a stronger urge for self realization.
A parallel societal ambivalence as well
on the planet, mutual annihilation lies in
dark shadows, glaring in politics.

XV

SOVEREIGNTY, a legendary defense of Self,

our innate inner thrust for being

often a bellicose bull unleashed,

a clash of horns, a two year olds 'no'

an adolescents rebellion, an adults

aggression at home, a country, a war,

often entanglements till death -

-the yellow and blue withstands

the red hammer's invasion,

threat of wiping out one's existence

as in Gaza, unholy armaments of war

maintain one's sovereignty, ultimately

the hero's mythological unchosen

yet ordained journey into battle.

XVI

REFLECTION in the clouds

a vast primordial sphere

home of dew drops and thunderheads

gauzy, filmy, frolicking cumulus ,

like prairie schooners on high

formulating their own mythologies

as they dissolve into atmosphere

A goat's head appears, a

glaring chimera, or symbol of

desire, whose desire? Mine?

Or only a cloud in passing

XVII

BRAVO for the Muse, its hidden genius

Galileo, Da Vinci, Beethoven

Tolstoy, Monet, Darwin

 sadly even Oppenheimer,

Bravo, until the Muse meets A-I.

Natalie Goldberg's first thoughts yield

 when intellect withers, when

the Muse meets its dearth

of imagination and intuition

and the Soul withers on the vine,

a last gasp of the mystical, the creative

genius of the hidden Muse.

A Requiem to the Soul, ah, farewell

my friend, my forever companion.

Deem it not neglect, rejection, or

dismay, only a demise ordained

by an evolution we hail and flail

only to yearn once again one day

for the Psyche of old.

XVIII

PUZZLING, the Invisible, the Indescribable,
a piece of the godhead inside each of us,
the personal within the interpersonal
words already diminished by use of words
a puzzlement to revisit time and again
confirming the Psyche lives.
In my youth we'd pour a few dippers
full of water in the pitcher pump,
prime it till rusty pipes awakened,
gurgled, groaned, and we'd pump
like the dickens till cold clear water gushed out.
The Psyche lives, the deepest of wells
Its presence nearer than we think
among uncertain faiths, unbeliefs,
amid the trembling of our knees.

XIX

PAIN and suffering, a karmic lesson or gift
common to all sentient beings
but what if pain ceased to exist,
would we need to invent it?
If pain became a currency of exchange
in the spirit of the Tlingit potlatches
compassion could be a gift of healing,
tonglen, the gift of giving and receiving.
Suffering raises our consciousness,
peels away layers between us and the Divine
and gives us grace to heal spiritually, thereby
the meaning of suffering becomes boundless.
Pain, an illusory phenomenon, cruel twist of
nature, a psychic clearing, or mortal threat,
symptoms we harbor like baggage
yet children ride naturally like unicycles.

XX

DESTINY, fate, chance, pre-ordained, or self-made

life's trajectory given, yet raises questions

What specifically am I supposed to be?

Or be doing? Or learning?

Wait!

Reserve demands, pause judgment

resign as your own analyst!

Know there's no fear greater than fear

of being happy, no resistance more

deeply seated than unwillingness

to see human errors, sins, as simply mistakes.

Destiny, to each their own, will become clear in time.

Or not.

Likely more vast and beautiful than anything

we have ever Imagined.

XXI

POETRY, the wind in my face
ta-da, galloping hooves on forest trails,
the flow of images shifting effortlessly
I laugh at the wings of my steed –
poetry in nature without words
the absurdity of thinking revealed,
a natural earthy language suggested
by Mary Oliver, Pasternak, Chris La Tray,
exquisite, their charming lack of guile,
their honest, deep freedom of expression.
I take the reins of the equine spirit
unguarded now like painting in broad strokes
word choice as limber as the wind
in my horse's mane and mine.

XXII

SOUL, quintessential illusive psyche

its antics alluring, our search foremost,

the journey pleasurable yet confounding,

ecstatic yet depressing, always the

the psychic electric drive

 for Being, I, Me,

seeking acknowledgment, understanding,

a reason for living, while moral stances,

temptations, waylay the unwary,

the bold and daring; still there's a path,

absurdities in all.

Above, golden light reflects a setting sun

in my windows, the Soul remains blameless

each of us Holy,

Who'd change it for a song?

XXIII

AUTHENTICITY, the real Self.

The fundamental truth about self.

How to become Self's second nature

in our consciousness and unconscious,

Identify it, name it, acknowledge

that part hidden to oneself,

Open Sesame with others,

open to sharing the personal,

open to unimaginable unity and love.

Love, our highest calling resides

in inklings from origins, from ancestors,

in the impulse for the immortal

Godhead in ourselves, quavering,

gnawing like droplets of spring water

wearing away stone, granite yielding

to the thrust of our true selves.

XXIV

PSYCHE-SEXUAL, semantics

a round-the-maypole dance

we seem compelled to name yet

grossly incompetent to label, or admit

 the unseen, unknown, the erotic

exquisite facet of our being

like one of so many red-eyed white baby

bunnies hopping untethered in the

Garden of Eden before the fall,

the shame, the countless years of

Patriarchal and Victorian ages,

our mythological inheritance

Zeus and Athena and Demeter

shunned only to arise in Freud's topography

through chaste medical terminology

until Jung and Joseph Campbell

bent sex and soul and psyche into

the world of gods and goddesses once again.

XXV

DANCE, the psyche a sheer delight

joyous transient moments, I exist!

Me, I am Me! Or a shadowy creature

of my imagination inspired to twirl

and fling myself about, am I real?

A fleeting body awareness, gift of

a capricious spirit in tune with the beat

in rarified air, a magical lostness

in rhythm and sound and rush

of tenderness and gratitude

artists feel in the flow with it

 writers, blocked, stew over it

impromptu musicians rap or jazz

horses kick up their heels and

dogs bark, running madly with it

In sync, in the flow, in tune with the Muse.

XXVI

ALONENESS, a sense of being too close

or not close enough, psychic pain,

being in that deep hollow of separateness

in the world, satisfying to some, distressing

to others more social; aloneness

companion to responsibility, sense of obligation,

fears of caring for others , of doing too little

or not enough, a sensitivity to energy circuits

enveloping ourselves or others, generated by

impersonal contact or relationships or lack of

a meaningful, mutual sense of belonging

a sense of plummeting energy

as if vitality is sucked from the room,

from one's Soul

XXVII

SONG of the psyche, Tolstoy's

romanticism of peasants

drew the writer to deep currents

of inner life lived only, truly

In the peasants' untarnished depths.

Walking barefoot In the snow

 among huts and rye and

small harvested garden plots,

the great man, so tender and touched

by humility, in contrast to the gentry,

died of exposure endured in his

journey into the psyche of common folks.

XXVIII

DEFENSES, wounded ego's sleight of hand

projections like movies on a screen

define every relationship and all unseen

coping strategies known to man

that mask who we really are, that

deny what happened didn't happen,

that adopt a myriad of substitutions

for failures, marriage and family, boss and employee,

for having been an abuser or having been abused

the psyche's devious tricks to save us

by a litany of means to ward off angst,

threats of annihilation by self or other,

all real or imagined attacks on one's ego

and sense of well-being. Tireless working

guardians lodged in the psyche

muscle in as stakeholders to preserve the Self.

Yet do I really need that phalanx of self-adapted

clever little muskrats to swamp my yearnings

 to be a free spirit?

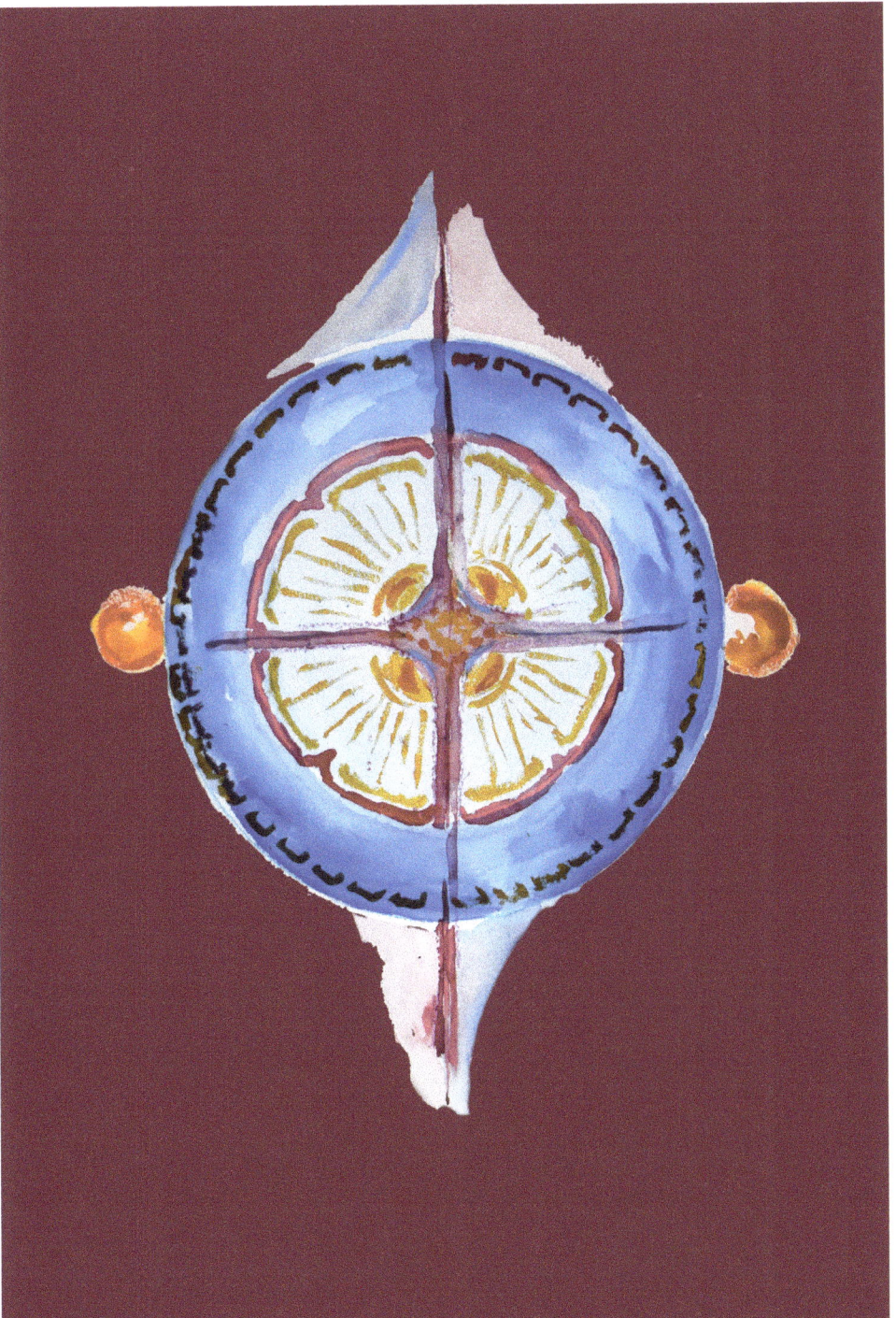

XXIX

DEATH by war and terror, the *zeitgeist*

of our time, death by numbers chip away

at our Souls, death, the common denominator

of refugees fleeing violence and war

death, less often natural with old age

as worldwide terror reigns out of control

mass school, church and concert shootings—

What am I saying? Death, school, church,

concerts, these words do not belong together—

the collective psyche of the world

has gone mad, split over justice and injustices

aggression, ignorance , beliefs and politics

Untold numbers sacrifices in artificial

 games of prowess of naked egos

massacres sanitized, the consciousness of

humanity forged into the unconscious of society,

swathed in downy layers of denial, the story

that shapes the collective psyche

that robs our Souls of their humanity

that drowns the wail of the people?

XXX

'WE are always arriving,'

the wisdom words of Octavio Paz

inspire a sense of journey

of leaving the womb, the cradle,

the pimples and pubescent moods,

loves won and lost, gambles won

and extravagantly forfeited to

inner longings soon left by the wayside.

Journey suggests arriving

birth, kindergarten, first merry-go-round,

vows at the altar, not being alone

on the journey of I, Thou, Me, Them,

until often bereft of health and mind

we transcend the journey itself.

Haikus Forever

In every being
Like butter hidden in cream
consciousness resides

∼

Inner self fidgets
Yearning, forever seeks a
dragon to defeat

∼

Storms of the ego
illusions, delusions thrive
Mystics understand

∼

Where go my senses
in a Universe of thought?
Whose dreams do I dream?

∼

Unconscious as Source
pathway of Divinity
illuminating

The way of mystery
spirals the way of the path
the way of journey

~

Threat of non-being
hear the wail of the psyche
perish or go mad

~

Forever seeking
to trust, to realize one's self
the tower of needs

~

Wisdom of the womb
Children forever seeking
what they've forgotten

~

Hail to friend Bacchus
Adieu to inner knowing
On pages of my Journal

Collected Poems

I am the unfinished script
the joy and sadness
in between

LEGACY

Bluebirds spring from stems of Oregon grape
flycatchers zip among tree tops
each cozying into nests in dead trees
in the Tetons, a gopher scavenges
for crumbs beneath my camp chair
the chatter in my mind stills,
acronyms Wi-Fi, TV, AI, IT
less relevant than the gopher.
D. H. Lawrence's bio lies in my lap
lauds his language of passion, vivid like the
river's incessant hollow drumming
to the heartbeat of springtime
with snowmelt from peaks
rushing to the forever sea
its depths beyond consciousness.
Teeming vestiges of a primitive world
plead as never before to be re-revered,
re-rediscovered, echoed by Lawrence
who made us look at the world
so we'd look at ourselves
to say yes to life amid crushing blows
of war, lost lives, and broken lands,
to greet the morning sun
as mushrooms thrust silky heads
in damp leaves and rot
while breezes lift the scent
of silver-tinted prairie sage.

CHIPPINGS

A glossy remnant of stone
among river rocks on dry hillsides
yet not belonging with rough
dark granites, sandstones, fossil-
filled sedimentary rubble.
Chert, I held the sculpted
bronze relic in my hand
willing its story to emerge
this day two hundred years
after flint-like stone against stone
chipped arrowheads from
its hardened fine-grained surface
leaving telltale fragments
signs, "I was here."
Impatient winds had swept
away soft moccasin prints
winds that turn days and years
into ages and ages of man
none more or less significant
only fleeting chippings
we leave behind, our stories.

DID I DREAM SOPHIA?

At once breathless with sudden revelation
Shaken, I turn to wisdom writings,
References spring from the pages
Astounding to me, the voice of Sophia
"I was invisible, now I am visible"

A dream found me in obscurity of the West
White iris in a green translucent vase
Banded with a ruby red rim under
languid petals, its stems metallic green
in clear water, the image puzzled me

A startling gift, my dream, the White Lily
Endowed with the Divine,
Grace, purity, the white iris revealing
The mystical side of the feminine
To me, bereft of help, comfort, peace

Lost to openness to the transcendent
I'd distanced from illusions of spirit
A youthful sense of the mystical
Yet revealed in dream when I'd given up.

Cheered finding Sophia resplendent
Resided deep in this wayward soul
A glimmer of hope pierces my experience
When I'd only sought a kinder God.

ALL THE QUEEN'S HORSES

Out of the mists of a foggy London morn
Beyond a damp cascade of red-tiled roofs
A welling rumble rose outside our window
Of iron-shod hooves resounding on
cobblestones of Sherwood Street.
A rush of dozens of sleek black horses
Rolling shadows four by four
Uniformed Guardsmen riding hard
Bent to the pre-dawn exercise drill
As the Queen's horses passed below.
A tourist's delight we'd never dreamed
My mother and I gasped at the thrill
As last ringing echoes of clattering
Hooves, now heard in memory of
All the Queens horses and her men
Encountered unstaged in mystical flight
A gift, a moment, a glimpse of royal life
To paraphrase the nursery rhyme now,
'All the King's horses and all
the King's men' aren't likely to put
The Queen's reign back together again.

THE HIJAB

Born in blood, live in blood
The hidden side of every woman
Lurks in the psyche of every man
Her power and yet her attraction
      feared
      exploited
Curse of the feminine
Myth of Eve.

Born in passion, alive in ecstasy
The psyche of every woman
Her second sight, aura of light
Fecund creativity, channeled spirit
      elevating
      joyful
Cursed with depression
Nature's cycle

Born to be misunderstood
The shadow side of every woman
Source of ills of the world
She wears blame like armor
      embracing
      nurturing
Subjected to injustices
Surviving

Wellspring of music and art
The creative side of the feminine
Softens and beautifies
Yet every woman hidden by hijab
    disempowered
    second class
Blessed with senstivity, compassion, and love.

I AM WOMAN

Breezes twist prairie grasses
a flurry of wavery ripples of rye
an equinox chantress sings
wild with desire to
the enlivened fertile valleys
meadows and mountains
glacier lilies burst through snow

A flame of golden sunflowers
innocent of face and form
yield to nature's incessant
deep wells of longing
spur a fierce drive and
interweave life's silken sinews
rich with sense of mystery

Not still, forbidden tide pools
forgotten in ocean's stony grasp
reflecting vain egos passing by
not a downy nest
cradling years past
not a lichen mosaic fallen log
nor empty hulls after thistles blown

As old as ancient wisdom tales
a pitted moonscape
yet climbs its arc of sky
and lunar's often cruel fates
tease nature's fantasies
besieging lonely yearnings
rich with sorrows of seasons

A long low aching earthy chant
lost in murmuring of awakening
of willows thick and trembling
gift small furry plumes
the sacred seed, the bud
the kernel of generations
and all that's ever been.

PILGRIMAGE TO ODESSA

Odessa, I pilgrimage there in daydreams

Of the mystical city on the Black Sea

Tracing footsteps of seekers, mystics

Questing the ways of unceasing prayer

From monastic elders, their *starets*.

Knapsacks on weary backs, the forest

Their home among aged tree roots

And earthly treasures only a beloved text,

The *Philokalia*, and handouts of bread

Sustenance of body and soul in

Sermons of St. John Chrysostom

Thumbed thin, translucent as

The Invisible, the Incomprehensible

Drawn on ancient Greek hesychasm

Contemplative monastic prayer

Inspiring a sense of sacredness

Of the World Heritage Site

And my pilgrimage to Odessa.

I DON'T REMEMBER I

I don't remember the in-between time
when being human opens to a dimension
in the universal unconsciousness
a subterranean stream of energies, thoughts
the substance of spirits and spirituality,
where unlikely as it may seem, we actually live.
Not so far a reach to feel oneself ethereal, a
wispy vaporous entity related perhaps to a waif
unacclimated to solid ground or food
or vagaries of heat and cold, wind and rain,
from that surreal time between birth and reason
before grasping the realization 'I Am.'

I DON'T REMEMBER II

I don't remember essential words

Lost to our family's vocabulary

Yet absent words shaped my young life

For a lifetime of identity and presence

On the world stage of pass fail

'Kind, be kind,' I don't remember

While 'Be nice, be nice to people'

Still a script, like adopting a persona

As if performing on that mythical stage,

I don't remember the word 'woman'

A split from my tomboyish self

its connotation being lady-like

Which I'd never imagine myself being.

MUSINGS I

Somewhere I read that people don't really

Enjoy living, not a prophet of doom, but

Observant of everyday American life

Mood and energy altering foods, drinks,

In search of healing, drugs, smokes, an

Addiction to Internet, all to deal with

Over or under whelming experiences

Of everything everywhere all at once,

As a timeless search for a panacea

When a Universe bestowed with gifts

Often reaps only earthly disillusionment

Subtext, expiration date expired.

MUSINGS II

Day dreaming, a contented indulgence

Without thoughts, itineraries, purpose

Other than living for the day

Musings, rambling thoughts, notions,

Poetry or song, maybe an urge for revenge

The unexpected everything everywhere

A half conscious state bubbles up

All at once, creativity, genius, yearnings

"I wish I could see my dad." a small boy said,

A day dreamer, not an errant student

I wondered how his life was after he met him.

MUSINGS III

Downsizing, everything linked to everything else

A memento as simple as a potholder

Sidetracks me, reveries trace a lifetime

The old cabin, Liza and John, crocheted

Red and white, hung on the whitewashed log wall.

Dutch and Blue Willow potholder patterns

Decorate my kitchen, as dear year after year

Gifts from friends, I'll keep them.

Grandma Elpel's red and green potholders

So thick you could reach into a forge

Edges worn and blackened

Save for another time of downsizing.

My daughter's crazy quilt potholders,

Long quilted strips of bluesy flower prints

De-cluttering arrested by potholders.

A MOTHER OUT THERE

There's a mother out there
Who glimpsed what integrity is
When my mother didn't press charges
Against her son who shot my brother.

There's a mother out there
Who experienced what love is
When my mother blamed no one
For the accident that took her son away.

There's a mother out there
With a grown son who has a future
Because my mother had a mother's heart
And not wish her broken heart on another.

There is a son living out there
Who learned from youth's carelessness
That instant forgiveness saved him
From living with blame the rest of his days.

A Tribute to My Mother
In loving memory of my brother

A heartfelt tribute to poet Jim Harrison for his prolific, honest expressions of the Soul that encouraged me to write freely if irreverently of my inner self. And I have to credit aging for ample time to get a clue ...

'*AUTHENTICITY*, the real Self
The fundamental truth about self.
How to become its second nature
In both our conscious and unconscious,
Identify it, name it, acknowledge
that hidden part to oneself, Open Sesame
with others, open to sharing the personal,
open to unimaginable unity and love."

Journals of the Psyche
J. E.

JAN ELPEL is author of two novels set in Russia, 1946 – 1986, a timely historical and cultural background to today's international events. *Journals of the Psyche* combines her interest in the mystical, psychology, and literature.

LINDA M. GRIFFITH, graphic design and layout artist for *Journals of the Psyche*, is a professional photographer and creative digital arts illustrator credited with design of numerous books and art works.

THOMAS J. ELPEL, publisher of HOPS PRESS, INC., is a prolific writer on ecology and sustainable living, and his venerable *Botany in a Day* handbook has long been used in classrooms and by individuals around the world.

www.ingramcontent.com/pod-product-compliance
Lightning Source LLC
Chambersburg PA
CBHW040242130526
44590CB00049B/4173